Burrows, Nests & Lairs

Burrows, Nests & Lairs

Animal Architects

LARK BOOKS

A Division of Sterling Publishing Co., Inc.
New York / London

Author: Ada Spada
Editor: Veronika Alice Gunter
Illustrators: Filippo Cappellini and Maria Mantovani
Translator: Amy Gulick
Creative Director: Celia Naranjo
Art Director: Eleonora Barsotti
Art Production Assistant: Bradley Norris
Editorial Assistance: Rose McLarney

Spada, Ada.
  [Animali costruttori. English]
  Burrows, nests & lairs : animal architects / Ada Spada.
     p. cm.
  ISBN-13: 978-1-60059-149-5 (hardcover-plc : alk. paper)
  ISBN-10: 1-60059-149-3 (hardcover-plc : alk. paper)
  1. Animals--Habitations--Juvenile literature. I. Title.
  QL756.S63 2007
  591.56′4--dc22
                          2007009269

10 9 8 7 6 5 4 3 2 1

Published in 2007 by Lark Books,
A Division of Sterling Publishing Co., Inc.
387 Park Avenue South, New York, N.Y. 10016

Original title: Animali Costruttori
by Ant's Books, Via Nazionale al Piemonte 40, 17100 Savona, Italy
Copyright © Renzo Barsotti 2005

English translation copyright © 2007 Lark Books

Distributed in Canada by Sterling Publishing,
c/o Canadian Manda Group, 165 Dufferin Street
Toronto, Ontario, Canada M6K 3H6

Distributed in the United Kingdom by GMC Distribution Services,
Castle Place, 166 High Street, Lewes, East Sussex, England BN7 1XU

Distributed in Australia by Capricorn Link (Australia) Pty Ltd.,
P.O. Box 704, Windsor, NSW 2756 Australia

If you have questions or comments about this book, please contact:
Lark Books
67 Broadway
Asheville, NC 28801
(828) 253-0467

Manufactured in China

ISBN 13: 978-1-60059-149-5
ISBN 10: 1-60059-149-3

For information about custom editions, special sales, premium and corporate purchases, please contact
Sterling Special Sales Department at 800-805-5489 or specialsales@sterlingpub.com.

Contents

Welcome to the World

Everyone wants a house that's just right—including animals. They design houses to suit their families' needs, just like a human architect would. This book is your once-in-a-lifetime invitation into the cozy homes of wild animals!

Go inside the burrows of prairie dog families and count how many rooms they have. Find out how they use each space for sleeping, eating, or relaxing. Inspect up-close the intricate nests of wasps, bees, and ants. See how some ants' bodies become like refrigerators for storing food. Imagine what it would be like to be a baby platypus resting in its cave at the end of a long, dark, underground tunnel.

Why Do Animals Build?

Many animals don't need houses. They can grow, survive, and reproduce without the protections offered by a home. But some animals need a lot of protection from predators. Most of these animals, such as field mice, birds, and prairie dogs, are small. Beavers, badgers, and platypuses aren't as small, but they still have predators that would like to eat them. And their young need weeks or months of parenting before they can take care of themselves. All these animals—and thousands more—build houses to have a safe space for their families. A house can also store food so that the animal's family will always have something to eat, even during seasons when food is scarce.

Some animals take advantage of makeshift shelters, such as holes in the ground, natural caves, hollowed out logs, and other hideaways they find. They might move some dirt or bring in some mosses to make these shelters more comfortable. But other amazing animals adapt to their environments by using their instincts and natural tools to build houses that are just right for their needs.

How Do They Do It?

Animals are born knowing the skills they need to build—this is called instinct. Every species relies on instinct to thrive where it lives.

Animals are also born with the tools they need. Beaks are good for weaving and sewing grasses, digging into the ground, and hammering into wood. Claws can dig deep holes and long tunnels under ground and through riverbanks. Antennae make good measuring tools. Paws are perfect for stacking and shaping sticks and mud. Strong, sharp teeth can strip bark and cut down trees.

Because constructing a house can be a long and tiring process, animal architects also need the right attitude. They're patient and focused. They don't get discouraged. They don't get distracted. Some don't even stop to eat until the work is finished! The building materials are usually straw, sand, sticks, and dirt. These must to be carried, stacked, woven, or carefully excavated. Animals might work for hours or months on their house. Why do some animals go to all this trouble? Their instincts tell them a snug, safe home can help them and their offspring survive.

Beavers are water-loving mammals that live on the continents of Asia, Europe, and North America. They have sharp teeth that can chop down even the biggest tree. Their furry diving suits allow them to spend much of their lives swimming in freshwater lakes, rivers, and creeks. Beavers work together as a family to build sturdy homes that can last for 20 years. Not only do beavers love to swim and play in water, but they can also use it to communicate. If a predator or other danger is near, a beaver slaps its broad, flat tail on the water as it dives for safety. This sound can be heard above and below the water. (It makes more noise than a belly flop!)

Water Lodges

Beaver houses have two parts: a dam and a water lodge. To build the dam, they carefully stack tree limbs, branches, and mud in the river. The materials must be stacked sturdily enough so that the water won't wash the home away. For the lodge, beavers build a mound that's higher than the water. Inside is a dry room meant for resting and giving birth to beaver pups. To keep out the cold, beavers line the walls with twigs and leaves. In winter, the walls freeze, trapping warm air inside. Each lodge has two entrances. One is for regular coming and going. The other is an emergency exit. If the dam fails and water enters the lodge, or if a predator barges in, beavers need an escape route.

Building Dams

Beavers build their homes in a section of a river, creek, or lake that shouldn't dry out in the summer or freeze in the winter. Beavers build the dam first because the dam slows the water's flow and lowers the water level. This way, it's easier to build a lodge downstream. Beavers stack the trunks, limbs, and sticks from trees they cut down, along with stones, making sure there isn't even the smallest leak.

Family Life

It's not unusual to find ten beavers living in the same house. Beaver parents share their homes with their previous two litters of pups. Pups are born once per year and up to four pups can be born in a litter. The babies know how to swim, but they don't make their first outing into the water until they're a month old. Pups move out of the lodge when they're about two years old. When they're three years old, beavers are ready to find a mate, build a home, and start a new family.

Chopping Down Trees

A beaver's only tools for cutting down trees are its super-strong, super-sharp teeth. To begin, a beaver pulls strips of bark off all around the base of the trunk. Then the beaver bites at the trunk, making cone-shaped holes. The beaver gnaws until the tree crashes to the ground. Cutting down a large tree can take less than an hour. But then the beaver has to chop the tree into smaller pieces and haul them to the dam site. Everyone in the family helps with the cutting and carrying.

The Beaver's Diet

Beavers eat leaves, buds, twigs, stems, and the soft layer of wood found beneath the bark of trees like poplars, willows, and birches. They need to eat a lot, so they build their homes where plenty of their favorite foods grow. To prepare for winter, beavers store branches under water in the mud near the lodge entrance. If the surface of the water outside their lodge freezes, they can swim through the hole in the lodge's floor and bring back the branches they stored in the mud.

Excavators

Prairie dogs live below the open plains of North America. They need homes that can protect them from many predators, including hawks and badgers. So prairie dogs dig out complex underground cities with hundreds to thousands of side-by-side houses. The main entrance leads several feet under the ground and then turns upward. It bends like this so that large intruders will get stuck or delayed when they try to enter. Each house is home to a male, one or more females, and their young.

Many mammal species build underground homes. This kind of work requires sharp claws and powerful paws for digging out their homes. Moles and prairie dogs dig elaborate houses that work like mazes to confuse intruders. They need many rooms for different activities and many exits for escape from predators. Rabbits need many underground rooms to house hundreds of family members, and their houses grow as the warren grows. Platypuses and badgers live by themselves and dig out hidden tunnel homes that allow them to raise their young in quiet and safety.

Sentries watch for danger at above- and below-ground lookout posts, ready to signal with a bark of alarm. (Their barking earned these small rodents their name.) The cities can stretch for miles and house millions of prairie dogs—plus owls that may intrude to nest and lay eggs.

A Dark Home

With their tiny eyes and ears, moles are almost helpless above the ground. But these small rodents are perfectly suited to their underground life in fields and pastures through-out the world. Moles have large webbed feet with thin, sharp claws. They're perfect for digging for earthworms and other insects. A mole can dig 90 feet of tunnels in just one day, relying only on its senses of smell and touch. Moles also have thick, velvety fur to keep them warm in the cool earth. Moles live in small families made up of parents and two to five young that are born once a year. Parents build deep caves with rooms for resting, raising pups, and storing food. They also dig shallow tunnels branching out from the home to hunt prey.

A Decorated Home

Badgers have powerful forelimbs and small, clawed paws to dig deep tunnels. These rodents make one cave for resting and raising their young but dig many tunnels as they pursue insects, snakes, and other rodents. In spring, badgers gather ferns that grow in their forest habitats. In summer, it's time for finding hay and long grasses. Fall and winter are the seasons for gathering leaves and moss. Badgers use their paws to collect materials, holding them tightly under their long snouts and dragging them back to their homes. These materials create a soft, warm space for young badgers.

A Warren

Rabbits can leap ten feet with a single hop—but their best protection from predators is an underground home. Rabbits have small paws and claws compared to other ground-dwelling rodents, so they build homes in dry ground on the slope of a hillside where it's easy to dig. They expand their homes, called burrows, as new family members are born. The burrow is designed with a large central room where males rest. Females dig tunnels away from this room and add caves that they line with grasses they collect in their mouths. The females raise litters up to four times a year. Thousands of rabbits can live in one underground community of side-by-side burrows called a warren.

A Hidden Home

The unusual Australian animal called the duck-billed platypus gets its name from the shape of its flat muzzle. These solitary animals live in riverbanks and have large, sharp claws and strong, wide feet that are great for digging tunnels several feet long. Whenever they aren't hunting shrimp and other animals under water, platypuses rest in their refuges. After mating, female platypuses dig new homes with even longer, winding tunnels and lay their eggs in caves they dig out and line with leaves. They also seal their tunnels with leaves every time they enter or leave. This protects the offspring from predators and flooding.

Small Nests

Dormice are a tiny rodent species that live in fields and meadows in Europe, Africa, and Asia. They have small, agile paws with five jointed fingers that they use to clear away plants and to dig small winter homes. Dormice can sleep there off and on for up to eight months. In the summer, a mated pair chooses a bushy plant near their favorite foods: fruits, berries, nuts, and insects.

Sometimes, having one home is not enough. Animals might need different homes for different seasons. In winter, some mice layer grasses in snug nests deep under ground and sleep away most or all of the season. But in springtime, they need a new house for their babies with easy access to food for the family. Insects like the caddis fly lay their eggs in water where they develop. Then the offspring fly away, only to return later to lay their own eggs. Each animal uses its natural skills to adapt to the season and its habitat.

Using their paws and teeth, the mice layer grasses as a foundation and weave long shoots of grass into a ball-shaped nest attached to the plant. They pad the inside with leaves and moss. The female gives birth in the new home. After the first litter matures, the parents have a second litter of up to four babies before moving back under ground.

Beetles

There are more than 350,000 known beetle species in the world. Some of them make simple homes for their offspring. A beetle can wrap one or more leaves together and lay eggs inside. Some beetles use their sharp mouthparts to make a cut across one end of a leaf and roll the eggs up inside it. This holds the eggs in place until they develop into adult beetles. After maturing, the offspring eat the nest leaves as a first meal and then find more leaves on the plant to eat. Then they make temporary homes under rocks, bark, or plants.

The Bark Beetle

Bark beetles begin houses for their offspring, but let the young finish the building. Parent beetles use their teeth and legs to dig a straight tunnel into the bark of elm and pine trees all over the world. They lay dozens of eggs in the middle of the tunnel and then leave. The eggs hatch into larvae that dig and eat their way through side tunnels away from the main tunnel. Each larva stops tunneling after reaching a certain length and nests at the end until it matures into an adult. Then the adult eats its way out of its nest. The bark beetles dig in a distinctive pattern to keep the tunnel paths from crossing.

The Pine Processionary Moth

Sometimes, when insect eggs hatch, a new house is needed as the larvae develops. The female pine processionary moth of Europe lays hundreds of eggs on a pine-tree branch. The eggs hatch and the larvae secrete a silky, web-like material that they spin into a soft, dense nest. They live together in this nest until they mature into worms. The worms emerge from the nest and march onto the branch in long lines to eat pine needles. The worms easily eat all the needles, killing the tree. Once they've have had their fill, they secrete another web-like substance and wrap themselves in a snug cocoon where they'll develop into moths.

Caddis Flies

Caddis flies are small insects that live half of their lives under water in streams, rivers, lakes, and puddles around the world. Caddis flies hatch as larvae from eggs laid in water. Some species collect tiny materials, including shells, stones, and twigs, and build homes for themselves. Their sticky, web-like saliva holds the materials together. Other caddis flies use the webbing alone to make a home. Caddis flies poke their heads and upper bodies out of their homes to eat plankton and other tiny animals. After the larval stage, caddis flies abandon their homes and fly out of the water.

Fantastic Nests

Reed warblers build their nests in marshy reed groves found in Europe, Asia, and Africa. The birds use their beaks and feet to weave basket-like nests from grass, attaching the material to the tops of three or four sturdy reeds growing in fresh water. The male chooses the location for the home. Then he chases away any competing males by pecking, squawking, kicking, and flapping his wings. Like a salesman, he presents his home site to passing females. The female that likes the site shows her interest by grinding up reed leaves and plant stalks with her beak. The couple then builds a strong nest that hangs above the water. When the home is ready, the couple breeds, and then the female lays three to five eggs in the nest. After a little more than a week, the eggs hatch. The parents feed and protect the young until they're full-grown. The tall reeds keep the birds and their young beyond the reach of most predators. The reeds also help them avoid the dangers of quickly rising water.

Most birds that build homes only use them for a few months before they migrate. Migration is when animals change habitats with the seasons. Birds will migrate thousands of miles in search of food, a mate, and a place to raise offspring. Unlike most animals that live in one territory their whole lives, migrating birds cover a huge range. Migrating birds fly north or south in spring, depending on where they live. When they reach their destinations, the birds build nests, mate, and lay eggs. Parents care for the eggs, usually by taking turns sitting on the eggs to keep them warm. After the eggs hatch, parents spend most of the long summer days hunting for food to take back to their newborns. By autumn, the young are full-grown and everyone leaves the nest to fly south or north for the next season. If the nest was sturdy, the parents might return to it in the spring. The offspring will build their own nests.

A Stage

The male bullfinch of Europe and Asia attracts a mate with his building skills. The bird uses his beak and feet to clear an area on the forest floor and construct a hut. Some bullfinches also decorate the ground with flowers. The building isn't a house—it serves as a stage for the bird during courtship. He waits for a female to stop by and give him a chance to strut around the hut. If a female chooses him, she builds a nest for their offspring in a tree or bush. She uses her beak to weave together lichen, moss, and twigs. The male helps by bringing her roots and more moss to line the nest.

A Fencerow

The bowerbirds of Australia are named for the elaborate fencerows the males build. Using their beaks, they poke sticks into the ground. Bowerbirds are known to collect all kinds of colorful or shiny objects, including bits of flowers, fruit, feathers, and snail shells in their beaks. They decorate the pathways within the bowers with their collections. A female that's interested in finding a mate inspects the bower and its architect. If she likes both, the pair will breed. Then the female builds the family's house on a tree branch by weaving a shallow nest made of sticks and twigs and lined with leaves.

A Houseboat

Great crested grebes of Europe, Africa, Asia, and Australia build homes on the surface of lakes and marshes where it's easy to catch fish. Their nests are houseboats that can be anchored to stay put or untied to go with the water's flow. Male and female grebes tear out clumps of marsh plants with their beaks and pass them to their mates for inspection. They weave the nest with their beaks. To anchor the house, the birds use their beaks to tie knots in a long piece of grass, connecting it to a sturdy plant. Both parents care for the young.

An Incubator

The malleefowl of Australia spend eleven months of each year building nests made of sand and rotting leaves. The mounds keep their eggs at the right temperature. The rotting leaves release heat, but if the mound gets too warm, the male malleefowl adds sand to it. This slows down the rotting process so the leaves give off less heat. If the nest cools too much, he scratches sand away. For weeks, the male checks the mound's temperature several times a day, using his beak as a thermometer. But when the eggs begin to hatch, he abandons the nest. The newborns must dig themselves out of the mounds, which can be several feet high.

Bricklayers and Woodworkers

Many birds make their homes by weaving simple, lightweight nests from grasses and twigs. Other birds have different building materials available in their environments. Some construct houses from dirt. Others tunnel into the ground or trees and build soft nests inside. Birds are all born with beaks, feet, and wings, but each might use these tools in different ways to help them survive and reproduce in their particular habitats.

No matter where they live in the world, birds build nests because they want safe, comfortable places to lay eggs and raise their offspring. The nests aren't supposed to be permanent homes. In the nest, eggs are laid and incubated, and the moment they hatch, the little ones are already developed. For a while, they depend entirely on their parents' care. But as soon as they can live on their own, the nest is abandoned. The more solid nests might last until the following season, and perhaps they'll be used once more.

Trees are scarce in the grasslands of South America, so a species of bird there called the baker bird constructs its nest on a post using mud. It builds its home off the ground to protect its eggs and new-borns from ground-dwelling predators (like snakes and lizards). First the baker bird collects mud and grass with its beak. Then it uses its beak and feet to mix the ingredients, just as humans would make simple bricks for their houses. The bird shapes the structure like a bread oven (that's why they call it a "baker" bird), with a rounded roof and a narrow opening. The mud mixture dries in the sun, creating a solid, sturdy nest that can survive high winds and hard rains.

Thick as a Brick

Swallows' nests look like mud pies stuck in strange places—in trees, on top of fences, in the eaves of houses, and inside barns. Swallows can build their homes in so many places because the nests are made of mud. The mud sticks to a spot the swallow chooses for its nest and then it dries, making the nest extra sturdy. Female birds use their beaks and feet to mix sticks, shoots, and mud, forming a brick. Then they shape the mud brick into a shallow bowl. Both parents create bedding for their eggs by layering feathers, grass, and other soft materials inside the nest.

A Riverbank Home

Kingfishers are named for their excellent hunting skills. These small birds live in forests all over the world and like to perch silently in trees until they see an insect, small lizard, or tiny fish to eat. European kingfishers prefer to build their nests in riverbanks so they can keep an eye out for fish. They use their long beaks to dig a hole into the sandy soil. Next, they hollow out a horizontal tunnel that is up to three feet long. Kingfishers finish their homes by excavating one room where the female will lay eggs. Hatchlings are fed fresh fish their parents catch in the river just beyond the entrance to the home.

A Hollowed-Out Home

When you hear a woodpecker tap, tap, tapping on a tree, it might be hunting for insects under the bark—or building a nest. A male and female pair work together once a year to drill, tidy up, and furnish a home for their young. First, they use their sharp beaks to peck a narrow hole that's wide enough for them to enter, but small enough to keep predators out. (The pecking is much easier if the wood is rotting and soft.) Then the birds drill into the tree until they have a vertical tunnel up to a foot deep. The nesting area will be at the end of the tunnel. The woodpeckers clear the area by grabbing wood chips in their beaks and dropping them out the entrance to the forest floor. The birds line the nest with soft plants before the female lays her eggs.

A Mud Nest

For protection, flamingos live closely with hundreds of their own kind. Year-round, they wade together in shallow lagoons and saltwater lakes found in tropical and subtropical climates. When they're ready to lay eggs, flamingos build their nests side by side in the water. Flamingos use their long necks and large beaks to pull up mud from under the water. They stack and shape the mud into cones that rise high above the water. The cones are solid except for an indented space on top. That space will hold the eggs. After the female lays the eggs, the parents take turns sitting on the nest and feeding the young after they hatch. Their long legs make it easy for them to get on top of their tall nests.

Weavers and Tailors

Weaver finches build nests in large colonies. They can build hundreds of homes in the same tree or bush. The male builds the nest with long grasses and leaves that he weaves onto a thin branch with his beak. Each nest includes a large room where the female will lay eggs. To protect the young from snakes that prey on bird eggs, the male weaver finch creates a special circular, facedown design for the nest's entrance. This makes it hard for snakes to climb into the nest without falling from the tree. Many different weaver finch species live in open grassland and woodlands all over the world.

Some birds build their nests side by side with other birds of their species. These birds might migrate together as a flock, too. Having neighbors can help provide protection from predators. With many birds living in one location, such as in the branches of a tree, it is more likely that at least one of them might sense a danger and alert the entire flock. The birds could also work together to attack a predator and protect their young.

The Long-Tailed Tit

Long-tailed tits are little European birds that build small egg-shaped nests each spring for their young. After breeding, a male and female pair of birds chooses a tree in a densely wooded forest. They use their beaks and feet to weave leaves and grasses together in ivy growing up a tree. The birds pad the inside of the nest with feathers they pluck from themselves and moss they gather nearby. The female lays six to twelve eggs in the snug nest. Both birds sit on the eggs to keep them warm. When they hatch, the pair feeds and cares for the newborns. The young mature in just a few weeks, giving the parents time to breed again before autumn.

The Common Tailorbird

The common tailorbird gets its name from the sewing skills it uses to build cradle-like homes for its young. The male uses his sharp beak to punch a series of holes along the edges of two large leaves. Then he collects spider webs or thin strips of grass and threads them through the holes. Using his beak to pull the strings tight, the tailorbird sews up the opening between the leaves. After the male stuffs the nest with grass, the female lays three to five eggs inside it.

The Penduline Tit

The nest of the penduline tit is a furry sack hanging from the branches of a willow or birch tree. The birds build their homes in marshy areas and near rivers throughout Europe and Asia. The male begins construction by choosing branches to weave together with dried grass, sticks, and twigs. The nest he builds is sturdy and has small branches running through it. The female does not participate in the first phase of work. She works with the male on the nest's final touches, covering the house with leaves and furry plant fibers to make it soft and cozy. While the female takes care of the new batch of eggs, the male will start building another nest designed to attract another mate.

The Smallest Nest

Hummingbirds are the smallest birds in the world and they construct the tiniest, lightest houses. In most species, the female does all the home-building work, beginning with choosing a branch on a tree or bush in a wooded area. Then she collects a few wheat shoots with her long, thin beak and hovers below the branch to weave a nest to it. The cup-shaped nest will be about the size of a walnut. The female lays two eggs and sits on them to keep them warm. Even the tiniest nest is strong enough to hold them all—adult hummingbirds can weigh less than a dime and the eggs are the size of jellybeans.

Multi-Story Developers

Ants are masters of making the most out of a small, shared living space. Their homes are called anthills or nests. Each has several levels of living space both under and above the ground. An ants' nest can look like a simple hole in the ground, an ordinary tree trunk, or a mound of leaves or dirt. But inside there's always a series of tunnels that travel several feet below ground. The tunnels open into rooms on different levels.

Insects that build homes usually need lots of room for family members and for storing food. For example, it's normal for thousands of ants to live in one anthill. Thousands! How can they do that without driving each other crazy? Their instincts tell them that a good home design makes it easy for them to live together comfortably. So they create rooms for each activity of daily life. Your house probably has a room for eating and a place for sleeping, and ants' houses do, too. Ants use their mouths and legs to dig out hundreds of these tiny rooms.

Ants use their legs and teeth to dig, and their front legs can be used for grasping or walking. They carry soil in their mouths and pile it near the exits, creating the huge mounds that give anthills their name. The deepest and most protected rooms of the anthill are for the colony's queen and her offspring. But food is stored in many rooms on many levels.

Food Storage

Nectar from flowers is a main source of food for many kinds of ant species. Worker ants collect nectar for the colony. They store the sugary liquid in their bodies. Their bellies can get so full that they stretch ten times larger than normal and look clear. The stuffed ants store themselves in special rooms in the anthill. When food is needed in winter or to feed the young, the full ants spit out a little ball of nectar. The balls are carried to the queen, young ants, or other ants. So would you rather be the ant that's spitting up dinner, or the ant that's eating it?

The Ant's Diet

Ants are omnivores that eat other insects, leaves, and nectar. They can even hunt much larger insects, like crickets. How do they do it? Sometimes the ants attack as an army and overpower their prey. Other times, ants scavenge dead insects. The ants bring food back to the nest, relying on their instinct to work as a team and shoulder heavy loads on their backs. While some ants hunt, other ants in the same colony look for plant foods. Each kind of food is stored in a different room.

Growing Up

The queen is the largest ant in the colony, and she lays all the eggs. The other ants are either workers or soldiers that take care of the queen and her eggs, and protect the nest. All eggs develop into larvae, which are helpless young insects encased in a semi-soft cocoon. Larvae rely on the worker ants to feed them and must stay at a constant temperature to survive. As the temperature changes, the worker ants carry the larvae to the warmest rooms. Following the larval stage is the pupa stage, when the young insects stop eating and hatch into fully formed adults.

Family Life

Every anthill has one queen, a few males, and thousands (or more) worker and soldier ants. The worker and soldier ants are all female, but only the queen can lay eggs. The queen and the males are born with wings, and they fly outside the nest to mate. After breeding, the males die and the queen returns to the nest, loses her wings, and lays eggs. She never leaves the nest again. Worker ants gather and store food for the queen and her eggs. Soldier ants protect the nest by working together and attacking intruders with their teeth. In some species, a soldier ant's bite delivers venom that can kill very small animals.

Queen

Soldier Ant   Male   Worker Ant

Termite Architects

Every termite has a particular job in its colony. Worker termites found in warm grassland regions called savannas build towering mounds that end in spires. They use their teeth, mouths, and legs to collect, carry, and sculpt the soil. The pointed tips are part of the air-conditioning system that keeps the termite eggs from overheating as they develop in nesting rooms. The spires catch breezes and direct cool air through the porous soil and into the mound. Termites also regulate the airflow by using their mouths to open and close slits in the underground walls. This lets cool air seep in.

Termites use their mouths, legs, and antennae to construct buildings that are millions of times larger than themselves. These small insects live in all but the coldest climates. Their mounds are working cities that house millions of termites and their eggs. Though they are only the size of ants, termites can build walls 3-feet thick to protect against predators. And they design an air-conditioning system that keeps the nest cool and moist. They also build roads, warehouses, and gardens inside the nest. Depending on what's available, termites use a variety of materials for building, including twigs, sand, gravel, and leaves.

Some termite species have indoor gardens where they grow plant-like organisms called fungus for food.

The largest termites are soldiers. They defend the mound from predators. Soldiers have armored heads and strong pinchers.

Members of the Community

Most termite colonies have a king and queen. They mate and produce millions of eggs each year. When the queen's abdomen fills with eggs, it expands up to four inches in length. She can lay an egg every few seconds. The offspring are workers and soldiers that mature in just a few days. The workers are the smallest termites, and they take care of the eggs and feed the royal couple. Soldiers patrol inside and outside the nest, and in some species, the soldiers spray venom at predators or attack as a swarm.

Queen   King   Worker   Soldier

The Termite's Diet

Termites are infamous for eating wood in people's homes and buildings. They'll feed on most kinds of plant materials, including trees, grass, leaves, fungi, and the excrement of vegetarian animals. Worker termites gather most of their food by finding it outside the nest, eating it, and digesting it into sugars. When they return to the nest, the workers spit up the sugars and feed the queen, king, soldiers, and the offspring. The workers also use their teeth and legs to plant and tend to mushrooms and other fungi in gardens inside the nest. If the weather is too harsh for gathering food, the workers eat and digest the fungi and share it with the other termites.

Different Kinds of Mounds

Using different techniques and materials, termites can build on the ground, under ground, or in trees. Some termites use their mouths to mix a paste of sand, dirt, and saliva. Then they use their legs to add wood and excrement—both their own and from other animals. The final material is mortar-like and perfect for piling up with their legs to create towering mounds. Other species build round houses between the limbs of trees. These need to be lightweight, so the termites chew up wood, mixing it with their saliva to make a paper-like material.

Defending the Mound

Soldier termites are usually able to protect their colony from other small insects, such as ants. But even a swarm of tens of thousands of soldiers biting and spraying venom is no match for aardvarks and hyenas. These animals can swallow hundreds of termites or eggs in one bite. The termites must rely on the thick walls the workers built from sturdy materials to protect them. The queen, king, and eggs live in the center of the mound where it is safest.

Aardvark

Honeycomb Builders

Hornets are large, social wasps that build their homes from structures called cells. The cells have six sides each and are made from wood. Hornets chew wood into thin fibers and then use their teeth and legs to shape the fibers into connected cells that form a shape called a honeycomb. Hornets are able to make the cells all the same size by using their antennae like rulers. They hang these nests from a limb or roof with one paper thread they create. Hornets choose warm places that are protected from high winds and strong rains. You might find nests under tree limbs, in bushes, on house eaves, and in attics.

Different wasp species have different house designs. Paper wasps leave their cells uncovered, while common wasps have large round nests with layers of paper that hide the cells. Don't try to sneak up on a nest. You can't! Common wasps build an opening in the lower end of the nest. Wasps stand guard there, ready to attack intruders and sting them repeatedly. Each sting injects venom that also puts out a scent that signals for more wasps to attack.

A colony of social wasps has one or more queens, a few males, and many worker wasps. The workers are female, but only the queen produces offspring. She mates with the males and lays all of the eggs for the colony. The workers care for the queen and the colony's young. Wasps can live year-round in warm climates. In cold climates, only the queen survives winter by hibernating in the ground.

Bees and wasps construct intricate homes using their mouths, legs, and antennae. But you should never get close enough to their homes to see inside because many of these insects are equipped with stingers that help them protect what they store there. Bees and wasps live everywhere on Earth, except in the coldest climates where flowers never bloom.

Gathering Food

Honeybees eat and collect nectar and pollen from flowers. They suck the liquid nectar into their mouths while their fuzzy back legs gather dry pollen. Honeybees visit hundreds of flowers and then carry the nectar and pollen back to a nest called a honeycomb. They feed some of the nectar and pollen to their offspring and store the rest in cells made from wax that the bees secrete. Hatched young bees swallow and spit out the nectar they're fed. The result is a sweet food called honey. Worker honeybees store the honey, too. The bees eat the stored honey and pollen in the winter when there are no flowers blooming.

Hive Members

About 50,000 bees live in a single hive or colony. Most are female worker bees, and they have the most to do, from cleaning and gathering food to defending the nest and making repairs. The males, called drones, mate with the queen. Then, most of them die. The queen bee is the mother of the entire colony. Her task is to lay eggs from which all members of the hive are born.

Worker   Queen   Drone

Bees Grow Up

Worker bees insert each egg, laid by the queen, into its own cell in the honeycomb. All bee eggs grow into worm-like larvae and then develop into pupa with wings and a head. After the final stage of development, the bees are fully formed and crawl out of their cells. Throughout this process, worker bees feed a mixture of honey and pollen to the offspring. Some of the unfertilized eggs become drones. A few of the offspring are fed a special, gooey food that worker bees make in their bodies. Those bees become queens. This food is also what worker bees feed their queens. So, it has a fancy name: royal jelly.

A Hole in the Ground

Bumblebees build their homes under the ground near flowers they'll eat from. In the spring, the queen wakes and digs a deep hole that she lines with grass and moss. Then the queen secretes wax and builds tall, rounded cells to hold the eggs she is carrying. The eggs grow into workers that dig to expand the hole and build more cells for more eggs, including a new queen. Drones are born in the summer, and they mate with the new queen.

Coral Reefs

Corals are tiny marine animals found in the warmest parts of the Pacific, Indian, and Atlantic oceans. Hard, bony skeletons protect their soft bodies, which are called polyps. Corals grow by dividing, so new corals appear beside and on top of the old. Over the course of millions of years, as new corals add themselves to dead ones, their skeletons can build up into huge reefs.

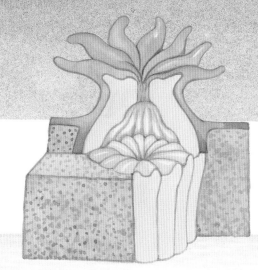

Coral Polyps

A polyp has a mouth for eating plankton, but the mouth also expels eggs and sperm into the water. This is one of the ways the polyps reproduce. The larva can swim around for weeks before attaching to the place that will become its home and where it will develop into a polyp.

The Great Barrier Reef

This immense ridge of rocks and sand is a collection of coral reefs along the Australian coast. It's more than 1,250 miles long and covers an area of 135,000 square miles. Imagine how many billions of coral skeletons that is! Other sea life, such as algae, can help hold all the coral together.

Coral Eaters

Believe it or not, there are lots of animals that think coral looks good to eat. For example, the parrotfish likes to eat coral polyps. To do so, it has to scrape away the hard parts of the coral—with its mouth! (Luckily, its mouth, unlike ours, is hard and beak-like.) But coral's biggest predator doesn't have teeth. A species of starfish called the crown of thorns eats coral, skeleton-house and all, without taking a bite. How does it do it? The starfish expels its stomach and wraps it around the coral. Gastric juices dissolve the coral until a part separates from its base. The starfish then sucks its stomach back into its body, pulling the detached coral inside.

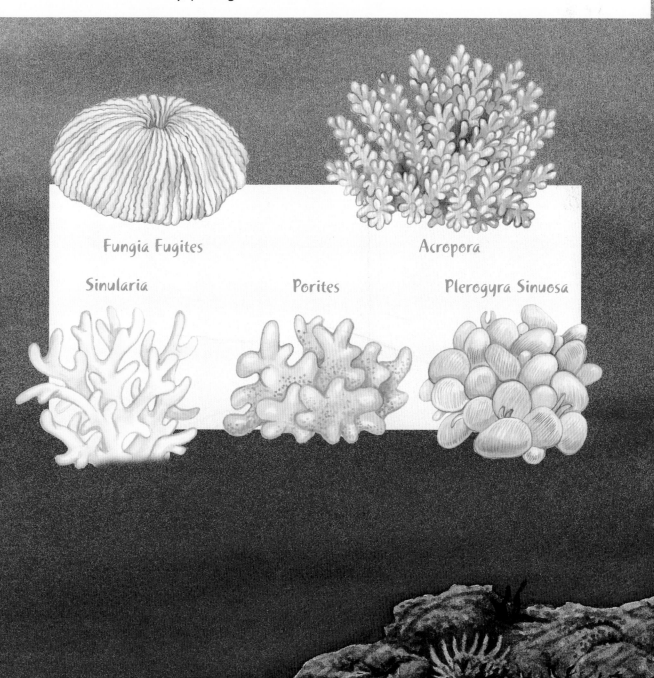

Fungia Fugites

Acropora

Sinularia

Porites

Plerogyra Sinuosa

Glossary

Abdomen. In insects, the last section of the body. In mammals, the area between the chest and hips.

Algae. Organisms that grow in the water and feed by photosynthesis but are not plants.

Antennae. Long, thin organs on the head of an insect, used for touching, smelling, or other ways of sensing.

Beak. The horny mouth of an animal. Birds often use beaks for pecking and pinching.

Beetle. An insect of any size with a mouth that can bite and hard wings that cover the soft ones when not in flight.

Bower. A private enclosure.

Breed. To reproduce by giving birth or laying eggs.

Burrow. A tunnel dug in the ground by a small animal that lives or hides in it.

Cell. In a honeycomb, one of the small, six-sided spaces with walls of wax.

Claw. Pointed, curved, horn-like material on the end of an animal's toe.

Climate. An area's temperature, rainfall, snowfall, wind, and other weather conditions.

Cocoon. The protective case of silky material an insect larva spins around itself.

Colony. A group of the same kind of organisms living together.

Dam. A barrier built by beavers to stop the flow of water and create a pond.

Develop. To grow, expand, become more complete.

Drone. A male insect that mates with the queen, does no other work, and cannot sting.

Egg. The female reproductive cell. When eggs combine with sperm, the male reproductive cell, they become fertile and can grow into offspring.

Fertilize. When female and male reproductive cells—egg and sperm—combine and develop into offspring.

Fiber. Long, thread-thin material.

Fungi. Molds, mushrooms, and other organisms that use spores to reproduce.

Habitat. The area where an organism naturally lives.

Hatch. When young mature and emerge from an egg.

Hibernate. When an animal's activity, body temperature, breathing, and heart rate slow to a sleep-like state to help it survive the cold and food shortages of winter.

Honeycomb. Many six-sided wax cells that hold bees' honey and larvae, or a structure with the same pattern.

Horizontal. Goes across or side to side rather than up and down.

Incubate. Keeping eggs warm until they are ready to hatch.

Instinct. A way animals naturally know to behave that helps them live in their particular environment.

Lagoon. Shallow water with an island, reef, or other separation between it and the sea.

Larva. The first, immature stage of insect development, when the insect often looks worm-like and does not yet have wings.

Litter. A group of offspring that are born together at one time.

Lodge. A place where a group of animals live, such as beavers' domed homes built of branches and mud.

Marine. Lives in the sea.

Mate. The animal that breeds with another. Or, the act of breeding: the interaction between a male and a female that allows the female to become pregnant and give birth to or lay offspring.

Mature. Fully developed. To grow.

Migrate. When animals travel from one place to another at certain times of year, often to find warmer weather or more food.

Mound. A pile, such as the hill of dirt made by the ants that live inside.

Muzzle. The snout, or front part of the head.

Nectar. The sweet liquid that flowers make to attract insects and other pollinators.

Nest. A shelter, often for young, built by insects, birds, or other animals.

Offspring. A new organism produced by reproduction.

Omnivore. An organism that eats both animals and plants.

Plankton. Groups of algae, protozoa, bacteria, and other tiny organisms that float in water and are eaten by many animals.

Pollen. A powder of male reproductive cells produced by plants.

Polyp. The soft, tiny marine animal inside the hard skeleton of coral.

Predator. An animal that eats other animals.

Pupa. The second stage of an insect's development after the larval stage, when the insect often creates a cocoon.

Queen. The egg-laying female in a colony of insects.

Range. The area in which an animal travels, hunts or forages, and lives.

Reef. A build-up of many, many corals (tiny marine animals with hard skeletons).

Savanna. A warm, flat grassland.

Soldier. An insect that does not breed and uses its powerful jaws to fight off threats to the colony.

Species. A kind or category of organisms that can breed with each other.

Sperm. The male reproductive cell. When sperm combines with an egg, the female reproductive cell, the egg becomes fertile and can grow into offspring.

Spire. A shape that gets narrower as it goes upward and comes to a point.

Subtropical. Regions that border the tropics.

Swarm. Many insects or other organisms, moving in a group.

Territory. The area occupied, and often defended or marked by, an animal.

Tropical. The regions on either side of the equator where the climate is the hottest and most humid.

Venom. A poisonous liquid that insects, snakes, and other organisms can inject by biting or stinging.

Warren. An area with many rabbit burrows.

Worker. An insect that does not breed and builds the nest or does other work for the colony.

Young. Offspring that has not yet grown up.

Index